"If you don't know where you are going any road will get you there."
— Lewis Carroll, *Alice in Wonderland*

Forward Thinking Advantage

Go from an Old School Manager to a Modern Business Master

Tracy Darchini

©2017
Looking Glass Communications, LLC
ISBN (ebook): 978-0-9988958-0-2
ISBN (print): 978-0-9988958-1-9

Forward Thinking Advantage © Looking Glass Communications. All Rights Reserved, except where otherwise noted.

To Kathleen, Jane, and Edith

CONTENTS

	Introduction	1
1.	What is a Forward Thinking Advantage?	13
2.	Your Forward Thinking Assessment	20
3.	Old School vs. Modern Business	23
4.	Trend Spotting & Voracious Learning	30
5.	Personal Branding	39
6.	Networking Online	54
7.	Adapting to Change	60
	What's Next	65
	About the Author	69
	Acknowledgements	71
	Recommended Resources	73

INTRODUCTION

"You must become indispensable to thrive in the new economy. The best ways to do that are to be remarkable, insightful, an artist, someone bearing gifts. To lead. The worst way is to conform and become a cog in a giant system."
—Seth Godin, *Linchpin*

Do you hear your "corporate clock" ticking?

That's the sound of time drawing closer to your early 50's—the period when many corporate professionals find themselves feeling vulnerable to being laid off.

According to a report by John Schoen of MSNBC News, " ... older workers are clearly making up a bigger share of the so-called 'mass layoffs' tracked by the U.S. Bureau of Labor Statistics. In the second quarter of (2013), workers 55 and older made up 22.5 percent of the large-scale layoffs tracked by the BLS — nearly double the first quarter of 2001."

In today's business environment, the ticking sound of our corporate clocks can start as early as 40. It's a sort of wake-up call that you might not be the boss's favorite up-and-comer anymore. That you're not getting responses when you apply for new jobs or promotions. That what made you successful in the first half of your career won't be enough to continue growing in the second half.

The subtle, yet growing, anxiety is only exacerbated if you're one of the many of us who watched our dads lose their jobs when we were in college during the "White Collar Recession" of the early 90's. Or if you are one of the many of us who saw an older colleague or two lose their jobs in the Great Recession of '08.

Timing was on our side since we were still young enough in 1991 and 2008 to bounce back if we were one of those laid off. But now that we are in our 40's and 50's it is a more challenging time to be unemployed. For one, vast numbers of younger pros are clipping at our heels as they outnumber our age group, and second, this stage of our lives is arguably the most financially demanding as we put kids in college and care for aging parents.

Younger corporate professionals came to the workforce with an advantage because they grew up with computers and devices in their homes and schools. When faced with a challenge, they default to technical solutions because they don't have a reference point for an alternative solution. They were trained to work at a fast pace and to come up with creative and collaborative ideas. (School has also changed a lot since we attended.)

While many of us have first-hand experience with some millennials demonstrating the stereotypes of "entitled" or "slacker", many of us also have encountered other millennials who demonstrate intuitive thinking, creative ideas, and striking confidence well beyond their years. We may not want to hear it, let alone admit it, but if we more experienced pros are not willing to evolve with the changes in business and society, we deserve to lose our jobs to younger talent who are ready to take companies well into the 21st century.

Competition is at the very heart of capitalism, and it is up to each one of us to stay competitive in our careers. A forward thinking mindset can be an important factor for building a competitive advantage.

It doesn't happen overnight, or just by reading a book. Like most everything else in life, it takes practice.

Over a decade ago, I was lucky to work for a company that understood the need to transition from an old school mindset to a more modern one through a massive culture change. A new president arrived with a vision that would bring the company well into the future, demanding everyone replace assumptions with questions to challenge the status quo.

Every aspect of the company was touched. In one year, the company changed dramatically. Among many other changes, a hierarchical organization became a matrix organization. Cross-functional teams were created to take on large and small projects in addition to our day jobs. Gray cubicles were replaced with bright open work spaces. PowerPoint slides were replaced with brainstorm sessions. Processes were streamlined. Everyone up and down the org chart was assessed ad nauseam.

Many of us in the company were, in effect, re-trained on how to conduct business, resetting our expectations for the company, our colleagues, and ourselves.

There weren't layoffs during the transition, but there was a voluntary termination plan offered to some employees with over a decade of service to the company. This was great news for the 30-somethings who could take a generous package and travel the world. It was also great news for those over 60 who were financially prepared to retire with the added benefit of the generous termination package. But for those in their early 50's, they were too young to retire and too old to find another job that even a generous package would be able to compensate for.

Midlife is no time to lose income. Many of us have the most financial and emotional demands on us in this stage of life, as kids go off to college and parents face the additional financial challenges of growing old. And then there are our own retirement savings to catch up on, as many of us have not saved enough money while we were trying to save our homes and our sanity in our 30's during the Great Recession.

But it isn't all doom and gloom. The good news is that those of us in the middle of our careers are uniquely positioned for continued success.

We started our careers at the dawn of the internet in the 1990's. We understand old school ways and have had to continuously adapt to the new technologies as they emerged and impacted our lives and work routines or be left behind.

Technology has been changing how things are done at work throughout our careers. More recently, those changes are happening at an exponentially faster rate. Today, not only is our daily work routine disrupted by new technology on an almost annual basis, but entire industries are being disrupted by people with no experience in those industries—think Uber, AirBnB, and Netflix.

It is not just technology making the disruptions. New business culture, most notably found at startups in Silicon Valley that create those technologies, are making a great impact as well. They are more nimble, faster, and in constant flux. This shouldn't be confused with being frivolous. These companies take business very seriously and recognize the characteristics of their culture foster success.

Most traditional companies recognize they need to change. Some may even want to change. Very few understand how to change. Some companies will try to change by creating a checklist of tasks, believing that completing the to-do list will magically create change. Others have leaders who think it sounds like a good idea but push back on actually doing anything to change. Heck, change is hard. It's uncomfortable. And people are hardwired to resist when they are pushed out of their comfort zones.

To stay competitive, traditional business leaders must transform their cultures and adapt to new business practices. They must set an example and demand change from the top down while also encouraging change from grassroots efforts. They need employees who are not just willing to adapt, but enthusiastically receptive to change and to changing fast. (Since everything is changing at a faster and faster pace, there is no taking the road to modernization step-by-step. It must be done in big leaps of faith.)

Today's business leaders—and even those on their teams—cannot afford to work with the philosophy that "if it ain't broke, don't fix it" or "we don't do it that way." There are other professionals willing to bring their competitive advantage to the table by suggesting new ways that technology can improve how things are done.

Those steadfast in their traditional processes are destined to have their careers ended earlier than they might prefer.

To be clear, this is not just "change for the sake of change". And contrary to the impressions some have, it is not just to accommodate younger workers nor to be on trend. The changes are necessary for a company's competitive advantage to stay ahead of the curve and relevant to customers' lives and brand experiences.

Much like the companies we work for, as individuals we must also adapt and change to stay competitive in our careers and relevant to our employers' needs and business practices.

Considering that, in our 40's, we are about halfway through our careers, it is of vital importance that we empower ourselves to drive our careers forward on our terms. This doesn't necessarily mean climbing the corporate ladder. Contrary to what most books on career advice for midlife workers suggest, it doesn't have to mean completely transitioning to a different career path or "second career." It can mean building on the years of experience in a corporation, organization, or industry we have earned so much equity in.

INTRODUCTION /

The way to continue growing in the second-half of our careers is by developing a Forward Thinking Advantage.

A Forward Thinking Advantage is the competitive edge one professional has over another based on the different value they bring to advance the business. The person with the advantage is the one demonstrating modern business practices—the kind of thinking and activities that are often associated with today's leading technology companies. The person without the advantage is the professional who is stuck doing business following traditional protocols.

Many hiring managers and recruiters assume that younger pros come with a Forward Thinking Advantage because they grew up using the technologies and mindset that companies are trying to insert into their customer experiences, marketing plans, and products. They believe that workers over 40 are too set in their ways.

Generally speaking, they aren't wrong.

Chances are, if you are an Old School Business Practitioner, you have probably been working at a traditional old school company for at least 10 years and haven't been challenged to think differently. Either the company you work for has no desire to change with the times or it says it wants to but doesn't know how.

Perhaps the company encourages innovative thinking, but leadership isn't demonstrating changes by example, at least not in a way that change is imminent. Because of this, employees continue to play it safe by sticking to what they know instead of taking risks to push for new ways of doing things. In many cases, employees don't realize that there are other ways to do things since they haven't been exposed to anything different than what has worked for them for many years.

In order to be competitive in the job market, each of us can't afford to rely on our employers to provide training in new business practices. Each of us is responsible for our own career development, even when our employers don't push for us to grow; when we are among the superstars at work; when we have been with the company for our entire careers; and when we believe we will retire with our current employer—even when our employers *do* provide opportunities to learn and use modern business practices, there is no such thing as a guaranteed job or a permanent one.

We must prepare ourselves for our next position, whether it is at the same company or not. We are all subject to the winds of change, especially in light of how unpredictable the marketplace and economy can be.

Technology, robotics, domestic and international politics, corporate buyouts, and just plain leadership whims can make for sudden and dramatic shifts to even the most established companies and the people who work for them.

Ask yourself:

If the company you work for announced it was moving to another part of the country and you didn't want to move, do you feel reasonably confident that you could find a new, commensurate job where you are? Or would you feel forced to move your family out-of-state just to stay employed?

If you heard about a job opportunity at another company that closely matched your dream job, would you feel prepared to apply for it today?

If you needed to find a new job tomorrow, would you be prepared to begin job searching? Or would you need to first learn how job searching is done today compared to the last time you went on an interview?

Establishing a Forward Thinking Advantage would give you the know-how you need to have empowered responses to these scenarios. Having a modern business mindset both makes you less likely to find yourself on the chopping block and better positioned to find your next job (or better yet, to have your next job find you).

It isn't for everyone. Some people will find every excuse they can to validate their stagnant thinking. If you feel that "I already paid my dues, I shouldn't have to change" or "That's not how we do things here" or "The job was easier before" then you really could benefit from gaining a Forward Thinking Advantage, but it might not be for you.

A Forward Thinking Advantage requires:

- a mind open to questioning assumptions and to changing
- the courage to share new ideas with bosses, peers, and direct reports who may not understand why there is a need to explore new ideas
- an entrepreneurial approach instead of waiting for directions

- taking responsibility for one's own professional development, even when a current employer doesn't push for it or pay for it
- an understanding that all jobs are temporary.

People who do not invest some time in their career growth and do not adjust with business trends as they evolve will go the way of the corporations that didn't adjust their sails with the changing winds, such as Blockbuster and Kodak. These companies, among many lesser known ones, assumed that continuing down the same path that brought them success would continue to work for them. But, as Marshall Goldsmith is known to say, "What got you here won't get you there."

Again, there is some good news.

If you are open to building a Forward Thinking Advantage, you will be leaps and bounds ahead of others at your level of experience, either because most of them are not aware that they need to evolve or because they refuse to.

It will also strengthen your position compared to younger pros who are unlikely to have your level of business acumen and savvy that can only be earned through years of professional expertise, navigating business politics and building professional relationships.

But gaining this sort of competitive advantage in our careers doesn't happen overnight, or just by reading a book. Like most everything else in life, it takes practice.

Based on my first-hand experience of over a decade of research, training, and practice honing my own forward thinking advantage, this book is intended to guide you to a variety of action steps that you can practice to move toward being more forward thinking. Combined with your years of experience, being more forward thinking should give you a stronger competitive advantage in your career.

This book can act as a guide to give you overarching philosophies and specific action steps to help you adopt new business practices into your daily work routine. Putting these steps into practice can help shape your business decisions and position you as someone with both well-established business acumen and a modern business mindset.

Whether you want to keep the job you have or prepare for the next one you want, the time to nurture your career is now. It is time to quiet the ticking of your corporate clock.

CHAPTER 1.

WHAT IS A FORWARD THINKING ADVANTAGE?

"If we do not create and control our environment, our environment creates and controls us."
—Marshall Goldsmith, *Triggers*

A Forward Thinking Advantage is the competitive edge one professional has over another based on their ability to advance the business through modern strategies and practices. The person without the advantage is the professional who is stuck doing business following traditional protocols.

The Importance of Having a Forward Thinking Advantage
Blockbuster, Borders Books, Kodak. Remember them? They did not adjust to the digital economy and were ultimately disrupted by Netflix,

Amazon, and Shutterfly. No longer profitable, these well-established companies closed their doors for good.

The same can happen to individuals.

If corporate professionals do not adapt to new ways of doing things at work, they can't help their employers compete.

As new technologies and societal shifts impact how we go about our daily routines—from shopping to driving to entertainment and education—businesses must change to accommodate customers' buying and product experiences. C-Suites across industries are trying to stay ahead of that curve, and they rely on us to help them do that. Some of us are lucky enough to go through a formal cultural shift program to learn how to do that. Many of us are not and must find our own way.

Either way, each of us has a responsibility to adopt new business practices into our projects, processes, and leadership style. In order to keep our careers on a successful trajectory, we must constantly be voracious learners and open our minds to new ideas and ways of doing things.

I was one of the lucky ones. My big opportunity to learn how to make this shift came when the president of the company I worked for decided that the company needed to be modernized and made a drastic and comprehensive change company-wide. Every aspect of the company was challenged to reconsider its standard processes, even those that had been working for many years, and to instead question if there could be a better way.

This was not "change for change's sake" nor just a lot of talk about change without follow-through. Instead, we analyzed, discussed, and implemented ways that leveraged new technologies, prioritized customer experience, and made decisions based on what would best prepare the business for the future.

It changed how I thought about business, and it prepared me for how I strategically develop my career for the long term.

One big takeaway for me was to take proactive responsibility for my own career path. In 2005, as a professional in corporate communications, I recognized that social media was set to disrupt my industry, but the company wasn't ready to take the deep dive into it yet, so there was no on-the-job nor external training to expand my skills in this area.

So, I took it upon myself. I made it my part-time job to learn as much as I could about different social media first-hand. (This was back when only teens and college students were on Facebook.) I followed social media experts online and learned as much as I could from them. While some of my peers were ignoring industry trades that were waving the flags of change, I paid attention to trends in the communications industry.

Because I invested the time to learn new skills, I eventually became the manager of social media at my current employer and feel more confident and empowered in the value that I add to the business than I would have otherwise. I have skills that are in demand and that makes me more marketable at 49 than some of my younger peers who are holding on to traditional communications practices.

I continue to be proactive about my career growth and would not work for a company that did not have a progressive vision and plan for its future.

Yes, companies can also have a forward thinking advantage.

Recognizing a Forward Thinking Company
Don't work for a "Blockbuster."

Some companies do not have the same sense of urgency to adopt new business practices. While it may be comfortable to work for such a company—one that doesn't demand change—we put ourselves at risk by doubling down on our comfortable positions.

Unless you are mentally and financially prepared to stop working in the near future, don't work for an old school company, because it is only a matter of time before what they do will be disrupted by another company or individual who will use technology to produce or serve its customers faster and more conveniently and cost-effectively.

One common trait of forward thinking companies is that their executives "get it" and, more importantly, demonstrate modern business practices by example, not just words. This is paramount to success because it takes all areas of a company rowing in the same direction to keep pace with changes. That is highly unlikely to take place by happenstance. A leader must have a vision for a forward thinking culture and demand that business practices be modernized cross-functionally.

There are a variety of ways that companies demonstrate forward thinking, which may include some of the following to various degrees.

Employee-Centered: Knowing that outstanding customer experience begins with an exceptional employee experience, these companies are all-in on developing talent and creating a culture that makes employees feel like they belong to something bigger than a product line.

Flat Structure: The company is structured as a matrix organization, not a hierarchical collection of silos.

Collaborative: Project teams are cross-functional and the workspace invites impromptu discussions.

Mobile: Working remotely on the job is permitted, not questioned, and is supported with telecommuting policies, mobile devices, and laptops. This can mean working from home or from the company coffee shop, not being chained to a desk or even a 9-to-5 schedule.

Transparent: Sharing knowledge, plans, and resources across areas is a value that is prioritized to the extent that it is almost tangible when demonstrated in brainstorming, project sharing, collaboration, open workspaces, and frequent communications.

Risk Tolerant: Encouraging employees to take calculated risks, forward-thinking companies celebrate failures as a way to encourage internally-driven changes, also known as disrupting from within.

Companies with a successful future ahead of them encourage employees to be forward thinkers and reward them for it. Some companies have been at this for over a decade. Other companies have only begun to make shifts to contemporary methods.

Recognizing a Forward Thinking Professional
Employees can't wait for a company to guide them through the process of bridging their approach to doing business differently. They must proactively learn about and adopt modern business practices, if need be. They must invest in their own career growth to make them more valuable to current employers or to prepare them for a job search at an employer ready for future success.

It is imperative that individuals take responsibility for their own career development, practicing modern business practices as much as they can. This way, they will be prepared to either help lead the way when their company recognizes the need to evolve or they will be prepared to contribute at a competitor.

You can recognize a forward thinker because they typically have some combination of the following key qualities.

Voracious Learners: Forward thinkers are avid fans of books, podcasts, TED Talks, iTunes University, and other resources where they can learn from leading individuals and companies.

Creative Thinkers: The person others consistently go to for "big ideas" is often seen as being creative. They are invited to every brainstorm meeting, and they are good at connecting dots that others don't think to connect.

Risk Takers: Often earning a reputation for being fearless and suggesting new ways of doing things, forward thinkers value failures as part of the process to success.

Digital Fanatics: A clean desk and empty filing cabinets is a sure sign of a forward thinker. Since they tend to use less paper and more digital assets, everything they need is usually on their laptop, including meeting notes and archived files. The forward thinking person is usually the one in the meeting who suggests experimenting with a new technology for greater efficiency and is most likely to be heard claiming, "There's an app (or a SaaS or other digital solution) for that!"

Intrapreneurs: People with a forward thinking advantage tend to have an entrepreneurial mindset for their respective areas, running their area of responsibility like their own in-house business. This includes taking initiative for projects that improve business processes above and beyond the annual plan of tactics and staying ahead of competition within the industry and outside of it.

CHAPTER 2.

YOUR FORWARD THINKING ASSESSMENT

"Age doesn't matter; an open mind does."
— Timothy Ferriss, *The 4 Hour Workweek*

While corporate pros under 40 (born 1977 or later) entered the workforce after the internet became a common resource, those of us over 40 know what it was like to work in an analog office. We have stapled business cards to Rolodex cards to manage our contacts. We have knocked the ball back into a co-worker's court using voicemail. We know the annoying high pitch noise of a fax machine in use. Many of us even know the frustration of not being patient for the Liquid Paper to dry before commencing on a typewriter.

We all left those practices behind us long ago as we adapted to more modern ways of doing business, but many of us have not fully adopted a modern business mindset.

A key factor in determining your likely job security may be based on how

YOUR FORWARD THINKING ASSESSMENT /

you are perceived at work—are you someone who is seen as "old school" or "tech cool"? (While most of the items on this list reflect a company's culture which may be out of your control, score yourself based on your comfort level working in such a corporate culture.) This very unscientific quiz can help begin to identify how you are likely perceived by others at work.

For each line on the list below, score your comfort level for each element from 1-10: 1 is extremely comfortable with the left column to 10 is extremely comfortable with the right column. Add up your score to find out how your comfort level with an analog vs. digital work style is likely helping or hurting your reputation.

Work at Assigned Desk	Work in Varied Spaces
Use the Company's Technology	Bring Your Own Devices
Work in Silos	Work on Cross-Functional Teams
Quiet Offices	Offices with a Buzz
Need to Know Basis	Transparency
Work Life/Personal Life	Integrated Work/Life Balance
Anchored Tech	Mobile Tech
File Folders	Cloud Storage
Waste Removal	Zero Waste
Cubicle Mazes	Open Lifestyle Spaces

If you scored 50 – 79: In all likelihood, you have been adapting to change in the workplace grudgingly and long for the "good ol' days" when office life was very predictable. Or perhaps you just have never been given the opportunity in your current workplace to experience new ways of working. Either way, it's time to take charge of your professional reputation to better ensure your job security for years to come. Look to expand your horizons by learning some new business practices, reading books by thought leaders, and boosting your professional image online before you get pigeonholed as a has-been.

If you scored 80 – 100: Either you started your career in this decade or you have done an exceptional job at adapting to change in the workplace as technology has impacted Corporate America. Keep it up! You likely are already tending to your professional reputation online, following thought leaders, and trying new things at work. If you haven't started establishing your authority as an expert in your field, it's time to consider professionally blogging, podcasting, or speaking at industry events.

If you scored less than 50: You very well may be the person who responds to every new idea in the office with "We don't do it that way." At best, you are probably at risk for being offered the option of a "voluntary" retirement package sometime in the next 5 years. If you intend to stay employed beyond the immediate future, it is imperative that you start opening your mind to new ways of doing things at work to boost your professional reputation in the office. Start by working on your LinkedIn profile.

CHAPTER 3.

OLD SCHOOL VS. MODERN BUSINESS

"The only two approaches to dealing with uncertainty are design and default. When you operate by default, your biology, which is wired for comfort, wins out and you almost always end up squarely in the gray zone."
— Todd Henry, *Die Empty*

For those of us who started our careers in the 1990's and earlier, we were trained in what I refer to as the Old School Business Model, the sort of traditional business practices that have their roots in the Industrial Age and became popularized in the latter part of the 1900's.

It's primarily what we think of as traditional business—think of Mad Men and some subsequent version of it. Men were bosses. Women were secretaries. There were martini lunches and golf outings to build professional relationships. Who you knew was often more important than what you knew. It may sound like a world from the past, but parts of that history are still embedded in corporate cultures everywhere.

Think of how work life has been portrayed in movies over each decade since the 50's: The Apartment. 9 to 5. Working Girl. Office Space. Up in the Air. Unfinished Business.

Depending on the industry or company you work for, there are varying degrees of how much of these traditional practices exist in today's workplace. Some companies stubbornly hang on to the old expectations. But they won't be able to much longer. Because new technologies and societal standards keep evolving, customer behaviors and expectations are changing, and business has to change in turn.

For one, women entered the workforce in droves in the 80's and 90's until it became expected that women would work, even after getting married. Many of women who entered the workforce in the 90's eventually became the breadwinners of their families. The impact that has had on society is not easy to measure, but we can be sure it has affected boardroom conversations and decisions behind work/life balance, family leave, equal pay, leadership, sexual harassment, hiring policies, succession planning, employee diversity and inclusion, among many other business topics.

Clearly how we do business has been impacted significantly. For example, we no longer have to wait for overnight delivery from Federal Express to receive a contract to sign, since we can do so digitally in minutes using DocuSign. The assessment in Chapter 2 speaks about how we conduct our daily work routine differently in a digital world.

Changing how we work is not about catering to millennials. It is about staying competitive in a world of growing uncertainty.

For nearly a decade, much has been discussed across industries about the need to attract and retain younger professionals. Sometimes the coverage of this topic can make it feel as if this is the end-all reason for workplace change. It is not.

Friends ask, "Isn't it time we stop catering to millennials in the workplace and get back to business?"

What might look like adjustments to appease millennials are actually the means, not the ends, to keeping business relevant and successful for the foreseeable future. Attracting younger workers is not about pandering to the comforts of younger employees for the sole sake of making them happy.

Companies frame the vision around millennials because attracting them is the litmus test that an organization is going in the right direction. Being an attractive place to work for millennials means that a company is on the right path to being a sustainable business, not only because millennials represent a large population of talent and customers who will carry the company into the future, but also because the shift in corporate values is necessary to keep the business competitive.

For example, those comfy living room areas around the office aren't just fun decor. They serve a variety of business purposes. For one, they provide an environment that encourages impromptu collaborative discussions between teams, potentially resulting in more cohesive and creative plans through interdepartmental discussions.

And that open floor plan? It isn't just to save costs on building out closed office spaces. While much has been discussed about the downsides of open office space, the advantages include a design that reflects a transparent culture and a shared energetic buzz of activity between teams.

If working in open offices seems like an adjustment, just wait for what the future likely holds: no assigned desks. It's sometimes called "hoteling" where workspaces are open to whoever is working in the office on any given day. With an increasingly mobile workforce, hoteling will make sense for some companies sooner than later.

David Burkus writes about how widely accepted principles of business management are being upended by leading organizations in his book *Under New Management* (a book I recommend to learn how to manage forward). "Corporate leaders, entrepreneurs, and organizational psychologists have been working to build a new set of tools—the new kind of management that managers need. They are challenging assumptions, questioning traditions, and abandoning so-called best practices," says Burkus.

He goes on to encourage managers to challenge the things most companies have taken for granted—organizational structures, vacation policies, email usage.

Before managers can begin leading their teams with a forward management style, though, the leaders must first accept the value of their teams being forward thinking and practice it first-hand in their daily work routines. Does it come naturally to you? What would you do in these situations?

These are just a few simple examples of how being a forward thinker is a mindset. What's your first inclination when faced with how to do something? (Not only in the office but also in your personal life.) That mindset is achieved by first being open to trying new ways of doing things and then through constant practice of different actions, from the tools you use to expectations and standards you have for yourself and your team.

At the core, just changing behaviors at work isn't enough to make an authentic adjustment. Our actions are determined by the values we hold at the corporate level and individual level. This is not an exhaustive list, but generally speaking, modern workplaces share most, if not all, of these ten values from the top of the org chart down.

Old School Values	Modern Values
Hierarchical Organization	Matrix Organization
Top-Down Solutions	Employee-Driven Solutions
Need to Know Basis	Transparency
Customer Satisfaction	Customer Experience
Risk Adversity	Fail Forward
Conformity	Team of Unicorns
Yes Men Mentality	Creative Thinking
Work Time/Personal Time	Integrated Work/Life Balance
Climb Ladder	Advance on Road Less Taken
Process-Driven	Agility

If you feel that companies are pandering to millennials too much, it is likely that you are holding on to traditional business values that served you well over the years, especially if you have been working for a company that shared those values.

However, what worked up until now will not work for much longer, because companies are changing how their values to stay competitive. Not because it is a fashionable trend. Not for the sake of giving millennials what they want. But because these values have intrinsic competitive advantages.

Unless you are prepared for retirement in the near future, it is critical to adopt modern business values to be faster, more creative, and able to pivot ahead of the competition—both the company's competition for profit and your competition for income.

While the general perception of those of us over 40 years old is that we are set in our ways and inflexible to adopt new ways of doing things, the good news is that each of us decides if that is true for us or not.

All that is required from you is the curiosity, desire, and willingness to learn and evolve.

More good news—to be clear, you are not to aspire to become just like a younger pro. Those of us between the Baby Boomers and Millennials have a special vantage point which allows us to offer a unique perspective.

We have straddled both worlds—the analog office and the digital workplace. Do not underestimate the power of this advantage.

We are in a generation between older and younger co-workers, customers, and business partners. By understanding the gaps between these generations, we can establish the important position of communicating and building relationships with them based on first-hand experiences shared with both.

What might be different for you professionally if you used this advantage tomorrow?

How might you become more indispensable at work over the next five years by using this experience to benefit the business and boosting your competitive advantage?

CHAPTER 4.

TREND SPOTTING & VORACIOUS LEARNING

"Learn. Unlearn. (Repeat.) Rather than viewing change as an aberration, we understand it as a natural part of the organization's development."
— Nilofer Merchant, *11 Rules for Creating Value in the #SocialEra*

Finding a job over 40 is no small feat. Employers want to know how you think and if you understand the big picture based on what is relevant in business today and what is coming next that may impact business.

What will help set you apart from others going for the same jobs? How you think.

How will you keep your thinking fresh, strategic, creative? Not by focusing only on your job day-in and day-out. Not by staying in your comfort zone. Certainly not by doing things the same way you have always done, even if those ways work perfectly fine.

You must practice being a voracious learner. The more insatiable your curiosity, the better.

When we started our careers, we had limited resources for learning. There were training seminars, mentorships, and subscriptions to business news publications. To learn from thought leaders, we bought books. Back in the day, some of us might even have had access to more exclusive information resources through our employers, such as a subscription to Lexis-Nexis or a Bloomberg terminal.

Today, Modern Business Masters have far more accessible tools that help them learn. We even have greater access to people we admire. We have apps that aggregate relevant news and information. Even the concept of mentorships has expanded.

Something as simple as using today's tools to stay informed of business news and information can make a big difference in being perceived as replaceable or indispensable at work.

Thanks to the internet, there are free tools we can use to connect with some of the greatest minds of our time. These tools help streamline the process of finding relevant and interesting news and information for us, saving precious time.

Before we go into detail about the tools that help to connect us with today's business teachers, a.k.a. Thought Leaders, let's first identify different people and organizations worth learning from.

Learn from Modern Business Masters
We are living in what is sure to be considered a historic time period—wit-

nessing the global community shifting from an analog world to a digital one. We are living in an age of business titans—those who are making that transition happen in its infancy, and thereby changing the world. People like Bill Gates, Warren Buffet, and Jeff Bezos, among many others, will be revered in B-school textbooks long after they are gone. You have access to them today.

Start by identifying the thought leaders, organizations, media, research firms and consultancies you would like to connect with and learn from, using this list below as a prompt. While there are far more than the ones listed below, such as those relevant to your specific field, this can get you started as you think about the sources of information that can impact your business.

THOUGHT LEADERS	ORGANIZATIONS	MEDIA
Amazon's Top Business Books	Boston Consulting Group	Forbes
Aspen Ideas	Forrester Research	Fortune
Fortune Great Leaders List	Harris Interactive	Harvard Business Review
SXSW	IDEO	Inc.
Thinkers50	McKinsey & Company	Wall Street Journal
TED	Pew Research Center	Wired

Modern Learning Tools: Apps & Social Media

Once you are done identifying the thought leaders most relevant for you, the next step is to identify the best tools to use to connect to them.

Practicing a forward-thinking mindset can help you stand out from the crowd, but how will you find the time to stay abreast of it all? These tools—apps and social media—help build a forward thinking advantage while also saving time compared to old-school ways.

Apple wasn't kidding when they promoted "There's an app for that." While many of us just think of apps as games, chores, and messaging, there are apps that can identify which business news is relevant to you, and then aggregate that and push it to you. Imagine not having to skim through a bunch of irrelevant information to find what you care about. Imagine that same service monitors news sources you don't even know exist? How much time might that save you?

These free apps are like secret weapons that can help you learn from thought leaders and stay informed of societal trends shaping business decisions, all conveniently free and on your mobile phone. These are just a few of the tools available and all you need to get started.

<u>Aggregating Trends & News With FlipBoard</u>: Thanks to FlipBoard, there's no need to go hunting for the news that is relevant to you. This app goes deep to aggregate news you care about and feeds it to you daily. It's a bit like Christmas morning each day as you discover stories about your chosen topics from websites you didn't know existed. Using this app may not only help you be the most informed job candidate, it may also give you a wealth of content to share with your network with the touch of a Twitter or LinkedIn icon so you can become a source of interesting news to your followers.

<u>SuperCharge Your Brain With Podcasts</u>: Imagine you had the ability to transport to a variety of speaking events featuring the top thought lead-

ers in the world. With podcasts, you don't need a teleporter or a travel budget. Using the Podcast icon on your phone, you can subscribe to business podcasts and listen to them at your convenience. In addition to subscribing to podcasts related to your industry or those focused on job search tips, consider subscribing to some podcasts that will boost your knowledge of trends in society, such as Aspen Ideas, TED Radio Hour, the BBC's Global News Podcast, Inc Uncensored, IDEO Futures, and The James Altucher Show.

Commuters' Delight With Audible: Most thought leaders in business have published a book. If the idea of curling up with a good business book in bed doesn't sound enticing to you, opt for the digital audio-recorded version instead. It works by purchasing audiobooks on amazon.com and then using the Audible app to listen to the books. The monthly fee entitles you to a credit for a book each month.

LinkedIn Influencers: Part of being a forward thinker is keeping your finger on the pulse of what business thought leaders are saying. LinkedIn makes it easy to identify leaders in various industries by assigning them an "INfluencer" badge. On each person's LinkedIn profile, there is an option to follow them without sending a request to connect as a contact. This will subscribe you to seeing the articles they post on LinkedIn.

Thought Tweeters: While Twitter has many potential uses, one of the most advantageous services it offers for career development is to use it as an information aggregator. For this intention, it can be used passively, requiring no time from you once it is set up. Open an account, follow the Twitter accounts of thought leaders, associations, and news sources relevant to you, and your Twitter feed will be filled with their tweets, many of which will include links to interesting blog posts.

Expert Tips With Google Mail: Unless you've been hiding under a rock the past year or so, you've likely been invited to download free ebooks, attend informative webinars, and receive must-have checklists and the like, all for the low, low price of your email address. Many experts share very useful information on blogs and through online coaching. If there's a topic you are interested in learning, there's likely at least one expert who is teaching about it online. Usually, there are dozens. The best experts to follow are the ones with whom you feel most comfortable.

Don't be shy. Sign up freely, knowing that most of these online coaches will send free tips and information to your Google inbox. (You don't have to use Google, but it does reflect well on you over other email addresses. Believe it or not, using a Yahoo, AOL, or HotMail email address will date you. Keep those for personal use, but get a gmail account from Google for professional use.)

Co-Mentoring
Traditionally we professionals have been advised to identify somebody with more experience to mentor us. A more modern business practice is to have a three-tiered mentor plan: one with more experience, one peer, and one with less experience.

Most seasoned pros understand how a traditional mentorship works and value having a more experienced person to admire and learn from, even through the second half of their careers. We may have even informally experienced peer mentorship—somebody who provides us with mutual support and who acts as a sounding board for ideas, processes, and career development.

But most people are less familiar with being mentored by a less experienced pro.

When I had only seven years of experience in media relations, the manager jobs I searched for required at least 10 years of experience. As my experience grew, the same manager jobs start requiring fewer years of experience. The jobs I had been too green for, I was now too experienced for. My friends experienced similar situations, as did numerous others I read about in the news.

It doesn't take a rocket scientist to figure out that this is one way companies can legally exclude older workers from consideration.

Conventional wisdom would have us believe companies look for younger talent because 1) they usually demand lower salaries than older workers; 2) they are perceived to be savvier with technology, and 3) they better reflect the company's image of its corporate brand.

While this may seem disheartening for those of us over 40, there are real advantages for us in this situation.

In looking to fill middle and senior management positions, hiring managers need someone who not only has the right skills required to do the job, but also the business acumen to navigate professional relationships and politics up and down the org chart.

While seasoned pros can learn what younger pros know, younger pros can

not instantly attain our level of acumen since it can only be earned through years of experience.

There are no shortcuts to understanding how to navigate the landmines of corporate politics. Or how to motivate a team to top performance. Or how to ride the waves of economic cycles. Or how to build critical relationships with business partners.

By offering a younger professional the opportunity to co-mentor with you, you are offering a mutually beneficial relationship to them. In return for sharing your experience to provide them guidance on their career path, they will give you insight to their perspective. They can be your resource of information for how to identify potential solutions—using new perspectives and technology—to address business problems and projects.

You won't agree with everything a younger mentor says or does, and that is perfectly fine. You shouldn't try to adopt everything they exemplify to try to act younger.

Ask for their opinions. Listen to their thought process. Observe their behaviors.

Then ask yourself:

- What assumptions do I make that they don't?
- What resources do they use for shortcuts?
- What do they value professionally?
- What are some things they expect from their bosses? Their teams?

- How does their perception of their career growth differ from mine?
- How do they envision their career path?
- If we were given the same responsibilities, how would our approaches differ?
- What can I learn from how they think and act?
- What can I apply that might benefit my career growth?

Look for someone who complements your strengths—in other words, someone who is strong in the skills and qualities you are weaker in. Consider younger pros in your company or field or outside of it.

With many resources at our fingertips, learning is easier, faster, and cheaper than ever before. Keep yourself informed and creative so you can continue contributing fresh ideas and perspectives to your work while simultaneously boosting your confidence and making you even more valuable to your employer.

CHAPTER 5.

PERSONAL BRANDING

"Different is better than better."
— Sally Hogshead, *Fascinate*

Those of us who entered the workforce in the 90's were taught how to make a strong first impression to be taken seriously as a professional—a pressed suit, some polished shoes, a firm handshake, a friendly smile. Our professional reputations were based on how we showed up in person—our style, our manner, our work.

Today, our appearance and manners still mean a lot, but it is far more likely that the first impression we make professionally is happening online, not in person. According to a 2016 Jobvite survey, 96% of recruiters report using LinkedIn to find candidates for jobs, and 92% use LinkedIn to vet job candidates before an interview.

Just completing your LinkedIn profile isn't enough to get found and to stand out to recruiters or other potential business associates. You need a personal brand that presents your professional best.

Personal branding is often misconstrued as a bad thing. I've heard friends tell me that they dismiss it as being "too promotional" or "bragadacious." Still others write about how personal branding is disingenuous.

They couldn't be farther from the truth. While it is possible for people to manufacture a personal brand to misrepresent themselves online, it is rarely the case. Just like a product brand, if a brand misrepresents what's being "sold" (in this case, your expertise), it won't fool anyone for very long. You must define your brand based on authentic attributes.

The biggest challenge in personal branding isn't that people misrepresent themselves. It's that they don't represent themselves as anything special at all.

There are over 450 million people on LinkedIn. While only a small portion of those may be competing with you for your dream job, to stand out you must have a strong message about what you have to offer that others don't. Using generic descriptions or trendy business jargon will get you in the discard pile along with every other "innovator" and "out of the box thinker" on LinkedIn.

By comparison, imagine you became a member of a dating website to find love. You could describe yourself as someone who likes walks on the beach, but honestly, who doesn't like walks on the beach? How would that help other members narrow down whether you're a good match for them or not? If, instead, you say you spend your weekends on the beach playing Frisbee with your husky named Shaq, you have provided more details through storytelling — you are active, like basketball, and aren't allergic to dogs.

The same goes for finding the right match for business opportunities. The more authentic and specific you are about what makes you different and what you have to offer, the greater the chances are that you will find the right match for your career.

A personal brand is a foundation for building a reputation.

Building your reputation is a long-game. (In other words, do not wait until you need a job to start managing your personal brand.) Both in person and online, how you act, speak, and treat others will work for or against your reputation. While personal branding starts with you defining how you want to be perceived, ultimately, it is what others think of you.

What the Internet Says About You
Conventional wisdom tells us to avoid having embarrassing photos and information about us online. We hear "Don't post any drunken party pics!" and "I'm glad the internet wasn't around when I was younger."

While many people believe that recruiters are Googling candidates' names to see if there's anything scandalous about them online, they are more likely to just be looking to get an overall impression of who you are. What are your specialties? Who are you connected to? What level are you on the food chain? Is there anything personal about you that they could use to break the ice when they meet with you?

What the internet says about you is what will shape that perception to recruiters and business partners. While most of us know enough not to post embarrassing content about ourselves online, what many of us miss is that even positive search results about us can work against us.

Take Maria, for example. She's a respected corporate training professional with over 15 years of experience. When a recruiter searches her name online, he only discovers positive content—links to her baking blog and images of her experiences as a Girl Scout leader. But does this content reflect her professional best? What does it tell the recruiter about Maria?

What if, instead, because she has a common name, the recruiter can't tell which Maria Diaz she is on LinkedIn or a Google search? Or worse, what if she had an uncommon name, and the recruiter can't find her online at all?

What impression might that give a recruiter?

How might a younger candidate going for the same job have a competitive advantage over Maria in this scenario?

Keep in mind that it isn't just recruiters searching for professional contacts online. Think about your current online presence. What impression might it give to the 30-something pro you are going to pitch your business to at an upcoming trade show? Would you be proud of the first impression it makes of you or would it reflect that you are out-of-touch with modern business practices?

Now, let's take that to another level. Let's say you have a strong LinkedIn profile, and you have curated your online presence to reflect your professional image. Is that good enough?

It is a great start, but I'll tell you what you can do to optimize your personal brand: Make yourself stand out from others you compete against.

By the time recruiters have shared a handful of resumes with the hiring manager, all job candidates who are invited to interview for the job have the skills required to do the job. Your mission is to set yourself apart from the others. You must know, and be able to succinctly communicate, what you have to offer that others competing with you do not.

It's a bit like ordering pizza. Let's say you're hungry and you are craving pizza. You see many different styles of pizza in the display. Any one of them would do the job of satisfying your hunger. How do you decide which slice will not just satisfy your hunger but also delight you enough to satisfy your craving? Like many people, you likely will go through a process of high-level elimination, a more narrow level of elimination, and a detailed level of elimination.

For example, you might 1) eliminate the ones that don't appeal to you at all—let's say, anything that's not thin crust. 2) Determine out of the thin crust options which style suits you best—you grew up with New York style pizza, further narrowing your options. 3) Select a pizza place that has the best reviews on Yelp. 4) Decide on the toppings you like best—ultimately you choose the New York, wood oven, thin crust pizza with sausage and olives. Yum! Mission accomplished!

Now imagine you are a recruiter looking to fill the Training Director position for the company. You receive dozens of applications for an open position. How would you determine which applicant is best suited to do the job? Like selecting the right pizza to satisfy your craving, you narrow it down from a high level to a more detailed level before having a dozen or so to send to the hiring manager for her consideration.

First, the recruiter eliminates all the applicants whose experience doesn't match up to the basic criteria of the job. Next, he might further refine the pile by looking for candidates who are local. Eventually, he ends up with a manageable group of candidates with serious potential.

The remaining candidates are all capable of doing the job. How will he decide which few to forward to the hiring manager for consideration? Due diligence. He will probably do a search online to learn more about them and validate the information they have presented in their application.

Among the candidates, the recruiter searches online for five of them and discovers the following.

- Maria, the training manager with a completed LinkedIn profile, baking blog, and photos of the Girl Scout activities
- Kristen, a training manager according to her application and LinkedIn page, though photos of her on Google Images show her working as a daycare teacher, not in the corporate office of the daycare company
- Reza, a training manager with an active LinkedIn page, complete with LinkedIn posts that link back to his blog about trends in education

and an invitation to connect with him on Twitter where he retweets leaders in the training and development field

- Jen, a training manager who has a LinkedIn page with no portrait and minimum information; also there's no other discoverable content about her on a Google search, despite having an uncommon last name
- Mike, a training manager whose online presence is entirely personal with a lot of angry posts expressing his opinion about the 2016 election

These candidates may all have the skills and experience to do the job, but the resumes that will be forwarded to the hiring manager are most likely to be those whose online presence reflects the professional image that was communicated on the corresponding resume and which best aligns with the company's culture and priorities.

If you only went as far as to have a strong LinkedIn profile, you'd still be far ahead of most pros over 40. If you actually invested in your career enough to create content that demonstrated your professionalism and expertise, you would be in the top tier of pros online.

But let's go for the gusto. What should be the first step you take? The part almost everybody skips—defining your personal brand.

Defining Your Personal Brand

You can be the best person for a job, but will you leave it to chance that the hiring manager will be able to put the pieces of that puzzle together for themselves based on what they find about you online? Or will you define who you are and make it clear to others what you do best to contribute to the bottom line?

Think of the most iconic brands that come to mind, such as Mercedes-Benz, Apple, and Nike. Their reputations are strong because they strategically defined what they stand for. Their branding is not limited to a logo or design style guide or even any one of their products. They defined their brands and then use that to inform their presence to the world through design and messages.

What a brand says about itself is a brand promise. When it delivers on that promise, the brand grows stronger. When it doesn't deliver on that promise, the brand reputation gets weaker.

In other words, a personal brand that is built on lies is not sustainable, because, at the end of the day, our reputations are what others think and say about us.

Each of us has the opportunity to shape that perception through our words and actions. The stronger our reputations, the easier it is for others to recognize our strengths right off the bat (and the harder it is for adversaries to tear us down).

Moreover, the purpose of having a personal brand is to strategically differentiate yourself from others being considered for the same jobs as you are—to be unmistakable. While many professionals try to promote themselves on resumes and LinkedIn with superlative adjectives to show that they are "best" they neglect to describe what makes them different. A list of accomplishments are excellent to include, but if that's the extent of what you have to say, it will not be discernable from the many others who are also describing their work with "best" and "most".

The Blended Brand Formula

So, how do you determine what your personal brand is?

(If you are uncomfortable with the term "personal brand," try replacing it with "professional identity" or "professional reputation" instead.)

Most people do not have a clear understanding of what their personal brand is, let alone have done the work to be able to state it in a sentence. Having a thoughtful and clear personal brand statement gives you a competitive advantage right off the bat. Just some of the advantages include setting you apart from other candidates going for the same jobs clarifying for recruiters if you are a good match for the jobs they are trying to fill attracting unsolicited earnings opportunities, such as speaking gigs or book deals.

So, with a shout out to Sally Hogshead for saying it, here's what you need to know about how to stand out:

What makes you different is what makes you better.

Your personal brand must have a unique selling proposition (USP), a marketing concept used since the 1940's that theorizes the importance of differentiating a product in the marketplace.

Since it is unlikely that any of us have one attribute that is uniquely ours, the secret to defining your USP is blending a combination of attributes together.

To identify one's USP, I created a ridiculously simple method that I call the "Blended Brand Formula."

1) Make a list of as many words as you can think of that accurately describe you based on a variety of categories, including:

- Experience
- Skills
- Accomplishments/Awards
- Passions
- Values
- Strengths
- Goals
- Feedback from Annual Reviews and 360-degree Surveys
- Compliments from coworkers and friends

2) Narrow the list down to the dozen or so words that you most want to be known for. Then, mix and match those selected words into various sets of three.

3) Identify the set that best describes what you have to offer that is unique.

Sometimes a gut feeling will make it clear which set of three words resonates best with you. If nothing strikes you as a clear winner, solicit some input by your trusted mentors, friends, and family.

Here's an example of creating a Blended Brand: My husband opened a food truck when we moved to Portland, Oregon, in 2013. It was a dream come true for him to make a living as his own boss cooking the food he grew up with in Iran. Naturally, based on my experience, I manage his marketing.

Because businesses don't have a face, they use logos to represent them. We had a designer create a logo for the food truck, but a logo is not a brand. It is simply a visual identity for a brand. (For a personal brand, your face is your logo.)

He had a name for the business, Caspian Kabob, but a name is not a brand. It is simply a name. It doesn't speak to the value of the price or the emotional appeal or the trust that is built over time. Ultimately, a company's brand is determined by the experience of interacting with that business, just as your name alone means nothing to someone until they have interacted with you or get an opinion from someone who has interacted with you.

We could leave it up to others to define the business, or we could proactively define the brand to establish what the business had to offer its customers.

To identify the food truck's brand, we knew two of the brand pillars had to be Portland (since it is a hyperlocal business) and Persian food (the product). But what if another Persian food truck opened up in Portland?

How would my husband's business be different? We decided we wanted the brand to be based on our values, and we chose "world peace" as a third brand pillar. Our story as an American and Iranian falling in love and our values of cultural tolerance made this an authentic brand pillar.

The combination of Caspian Kabob's three brand pillars—Portland, Persia, and World Peace—gave us a brand that no other similar business would be able to authentically represent in the same way. It helps to differentiate his business and to inform all of our marketing decisions. All marketing, communications, social media posts, and so forth point to at least one of those brand pillars.

What are three qualities you have that you want to be known for, and when combined, help you stand out professionally with a strong brand statement?

Social Proof
I find it very rare that people try to fake their images through personal branding, either online or in person. It is very difficult for most people to fake who they are for long. Eventually, their true selves come out. We can try to present ourselves as someone different than who we actually are, but people aren't likely to believe it without validation from others online, also known as social proof.

When social proof is used to support a personal brand, trust is built for that brand.

Social proof can come in the form of recommendations and endorsements on LinkedIn. It can come from the number of followers on your

Twitter account or on your blog. It can come in the form of being published or speaking publically. It can also come from an association to reputable third-parties such as being published or interviewed in top tier media or published by a traditional publishing house.

These are ways that someone who does not know you can begin to feel confident that how you present yourself online is authentic.

Let's say I want to fake my image online. For example, I can list "software development" as one of my skills on my LinkedIn page, even though I know nothing about software development. Chances are that few if any people will endorse me for that skill since I have never demonstrated it.

For the sake of argument, let's say I manage to talk a bunch of my friends into endorsing me for software development even though I have no experience with it whatsoever. At first glance, someone may be impressed I have been endorsed for this skill, but when they take a closer look, they see that the people who endorsed me are not in computer science careers. That's a very different level of social proof than having actual software engineers making the endorsements. LinkedIn's formulas are starting to help identify the level of expertise of those giving endorsements, giving more credibility to the skills we list on our profiles.

Personal Style
I'd be remiss not to mention how a person's "in real life" appearance is important in representing their personal brand.

You don't want to represent yourself online as five or more years younger or 20 or more pounds lighter than you really are when you show up for an interview. Misrepresentation online about your appearance will only discredit all else you have to communicate about yourself.

It would further confuse the interviewer if you present yourself online as a forward thinker, but then show up in an outdated suit and hairstyle.

So, here's my confession: I'm lousy at the whole fashion thing and your physical image is a very personal matter, so I wouldn't dare tell you what to do with your hair or clothes. Not specifically anyway. However, it is important that your physical appearance matches up with your contemporary mindset.

It's not about having to look young, but you do have to convey that you get today's business practices, and you can't portray that with a hairstyle inspired by Marky Mark or Rachel Green.

Consider conducting an informal evaluation of your physical appearance and adjusting as needed. A trusted friend whose fashion sense you admire is a big help here for a reality check.

Take out a picture of you 10 years ago. Is your hairstyle the same today? If so, you probably need to update it.

Tips:

- Buy three leading men's or women's fashion magazines. Cut out pictures of hairstyles you think may look good on you.
- Find the best hair salon in your area and book an appointment for a consultation with a lead stylist. Prepare to invest some money on yourself.

- Show the stylist your magazine clippings and discuss the style you have, the styles you find appealing, and ask what styles they would recommend.

- Not sure about coloring the grays? Whichever you are more comfortable with is just fine. Just remember that being old school is a mindset, not a hair color.

- The same goes for facial hair, fellows. The goatee you all seem to be compelled to grow in your 40's isn't fooling anyone into thinking you're young. And ladies, if you're in denial about your mid-life billy goat beard, it's time to take a close look in the magnifying mirror and invest in a top-quality tweezer or spa treatment.

One of the worse things about turning 40 was losing my 20/20 eyesight. If it wasn't bad enough not to be able to see clearly without glasses, it was all made worse that I haven't found a pair of glasses that I think look good on my face. Like shoes, glasses are a fashion item, and depending on the season and year you're shopping, you may not have much luck finding a design that fits your style. I may not like the style that is fashionable today, but wearing something outdated is a worse option, so I try everything I can to find something suitable for my personal style that's in fashion.

Again, finding your forward thinking personal style is not about trying to look younger, but it is about looking contemporary. Reflecting your modern business know-how starts with your appearance in person and online.

CHAPTER 6.

NETWORKING ONLINE

> "When you help others make money by connecting them together, the world forces itself into the Möbius strip of success that brings the money right back to you times ten."
> — James Altucher, *The Choose Yourself Guide to Wealth*

Business events can feel like high school dances. Some packs of people who know each other stick together in cliques, never truly reaching out of their comfort zone. Others sit on the sidelines like wallflowers, waiting to go home to their pajamas and The Tonight Show. A scarce few may end up networking with someone they end up having a fruitful business relationship with, but most of us are lucky to leave with a few pleasant exchanges and business cards.

Meeting people in real life, face-to-face is important for building professional relationships. While networking events still have a place in doing business today, our networking opportunities online are practically infinite and provide a much greater chance of success.

Advantages of Online Networking

Besides not having to suffer through another chicken dinner, you can benefit from networking online because it gives you a chance to be strategic about reaching out to people you are meeting. The old school method of trying to strike up a conversation in person when a stranger walks up to you does not offer a chance to put thought into the conversation in advance. The internet provides many opportunities to identify who you want to connect to, find out more about them before reaching out, and then gaining access to them through LinkedIn, Twitter, or otherwise.

Some advantages to networking online instead of in person:

- You can be strategic and prepare before networking with someone specific online, as opposed to flying by the seat of your pants with whoever happens to be at a networking event.
- Networking online has the potential to reach almost anyone in the world. It's not just limited to whoever is in the room.
- Networking online saves time in identifying those you may have a mutually beneficial business relationship with and getting to know them.
- Most of us feel more confident behind a computer than we do in person.
- There's no need to spend money or time away from family to travel to a conference in order to network online.
- After connecting with someone online, the ice is broken, and an offer to meet face-to-face for lunch or at the next industry event is usually welcomed, since the two parties have established, in advance of

meeting each other in person, that there is potential for a mutually beneficial, professional connection.

Give Before You Get

There is a networking philosophy that may not be new, but is often forgotten: give before you get. Whether you are introducing yourself to a complete stranger at a trade show or on LinkedIn, actively listen to them, identify their challenges when possible, and offer to lend a hand, even a small one, to help them come up with solutions.

When reaching out to someone you would like to know, remember you are looking to build a relationship. Compare it to how you would approach asking someone out on a date. Don't introduce yourself with a marriage proposal to a stranger. First, offer to "buy them a drink" or in this case, offer them some sort of service, even a small one. If that goes well, then consider offering them "dinner"—a larger, but commitment-free, service. Give it time. Make sure the feeling is reciprocated. Charm. Don't pounce. Eventually, as the relationship grows, they will reciprocate.

And don't forget to start by making sure your LinkedIn profile is at All-Star status because once you start networking online, more people are likely to check out your LinkedIn page.

Identifying Contacts for Your Network

Be clear about who you would like to connect with. Take some time to put thought into it. What's your purpose—to sell something? To stay informed? To know someone inside of a company you may want to work at someday?

Make a list of up to a dozen people you would like to know. Consider what you may have to offer each of them. (Something that you aren't selling! Remember: give before you get.) Dedicate one lunch hour a month to meeting up with someone you've met online, and you'll have 12 new pros in your network by this time next year.

Where to Connect
Based on who you want to connect with, identify where those targeted connections are likely to be engaged online. Start there. You may want to start interacting with them on Twitter or an industry association membership site, or on their blog. That can help break the ice before reaching out to connect with them on LinkedIn.

LinkedIn: Professional profiles can give you a lot of information on the people you want to connect with. Search for relevant LinkedIn groups to engage with your targeted connections by offering solutions to the questions they ask on the forums. Always personalize your LinkedIn invitations, especially to people who you do not already have an established relationship with. Explain why you want to connect with them, and then have a sincere conversation that does not try to sell them anything until a relationship has been established.

Facebook: Like most people, you probably only connect with people you know on Facebook. But did you know you can belong to Facebook groups without having to be connected one-on-one with group members? This makes it possible to interact on Facebook with strangers with similar interests without having to "friend" them. Do a search to see what professional groups may be there for you to interact with, including alumni groups from your schools and previous employers.

Twitter: While Facebook is a good place to connect to people you know, Twitter makes it possible to connect with people you would like to know. Listen to them first by following their tweets, and then engage with solutions to their problems. Use hashtags pertaining to your business to be found by more people.

Membership Sites: Check out the websites for your industry's associations. Some have amazing membership sites where others in your industry are engaged and eager to connect.

How to Connect
Sales pitches are like marriage proposals. There's no place for them unless you have established a relationship based on trust first. Offer something of value to the person you are reaching out to. This could be an invitation for an introductory lunch or an industry event. It could simply be an offer to connect them to someone else you know who may be a good resource for their business. (A discounted or trial offer for your product does not count as giving. It is sales.)

Old School Manners: Make your mother proud. Use the etiquette you learned in childhood and treat others the way you would want to be treated. I'm sure I'm not the only one who receives a dozen emailed sales pitches by people who write subject lines as if I'm supposed to know them, had promised them something, or downright make it sound like I was obligated to respond.

Listen: Follow your targeted contacts for a while before reaching out to them. What are they posting about on LinkedIn and Twitter? Have they expressed a challenge they are facing that you may be able to address?

Refer to their interests when you reach out to them to show that you are genuinely interested in them.

Show Relevance: When introducing yourself, keep it brief and make the reason for connecting clear—what is the mutually beneficial potential of a professional connection? What do you have to offer that may be of value to them that is not a sales pitch?

Follow-Up: If you truly want to build a professional relationship with someone, don't drop off the face of the Earth after connecting online. Make an effort to grow the relationship little by little.

Business is a vital part of our society and relies on interconnectedness. Building our professional networks helps to build our influence, our resources for support across industries, and our economy.

CHAPTER 7.

ADAPTING TO CHANGE

"The closer psychologists look at the careers of the gifted, the smaller the role innate talent seems to play and the bigger role preparation seems to play."
— Malcolm Gladwell, *Outliers: The Story of Success*

Change is the only constant. With technological advances change is happening exponentially in all aspects of life, work, and our culture. Our ability to continue to provide for ourselves and our loved ones depends on our ability to ride the waves of change, so we all need to learn how to embrace it and master it.

Years ago, I believed that I was not comfortable with change. So, when a former employer informed the entire staff that the company was going to be turned upside down to prepare the business for the future, I had to make a decision: either double down on being stubborn or learn how to embrace change.

I chose to embrace change. I decided to welcome it as an adventurous challenge. I decided to tone down the cynicism that had built up over many years of professional experience and to tap the enthusiasm and mental "blank page" I had earlier in my career. To some others in the office, it may have appeared I drank the Kool-Aid as I advocated for many of the changes to come in processes, culture, structure, and work environment, but it was strategic on my part in an effort to continuously grow.

Like most other skills, if you are not already hardwired to be adaptable, you need to practice it regularly to see improvement in yourself. While this isn't a comprehensive list of ways to practice adaptability, practicing some or all of these approaches to working with others can get you started on the right road.

Say Yes
Practice saying yes to new ideas. Sounds easy enough, but many people are still doing things at work the way they did them 10 years ago (or more!). They feel it isn't necessary to try to news of doing things since their way works. They often respond to new ideas with, "That's not how we do it."

Or they may instantly respond with, "We tried it that way before and it didn't work," not taking into consideration that many things have changed outside of the company in the past few years, if not in it.

If your default response to a new idea is to play Devil's advocate, try listening to the Angel on your other shoulder first to consider the pros before the cons.

Being prepared to say "yes" does not mean actually saying it each time a new idea is presented. It means being open and ready to say yes instead of jumping to "no" whenever something new comes along.

Plan B

Being open to change requires a willingness to be flexible. You can practice this by having a Plan B at the ready whenever you propose an idea or plan a project at work or in your personal life.

Planning a vacation to the beach? A presentation to the boss? A birthday party for your child? Consider some ways things could go wrong and some solutions for how you will handle it.

You likely started with some more obvious hurdles, like an unexpected storm coming into the coast on your vacation … the laptop not working for your presentation … forgetting the birthday candles.

Now challenge yourself to identify some assumptions that are less obvious. What would you never expect to go wrong? The hotel has no wifi … there's no air conditioning in your meeting room … the balloon bouquet flew away.

Brainstorm alternative solutions for such circumstances. Even when you don't need to fall back on using your backup plans, the practice of thinking through various scenarios will help you adapt to change in general.

Abundance Mindset

I once heard it said that hoarding is a reflection of not trusting Life will provide when something is needed in the future, as in "But, I may need this someday, so I'll keep it." This is known as a scarcity mindset, a term coined by Steven Covey, author of *The 7 Habits of Highly Effective People*.

Alternately, an abundance mindset believes there is plenty out there for everybody, and we will each have what we need when the time comes for it. It results in sharing and discovering possibilities and creativity.

To learn to get more comfortable with change, you can practice an abundant mindset by focusing on gratitude for what you have and reduce your consumerism. Clean out your closets. Reorganize. For three months, sacrifice even one thing you indulge in daily to see what it feels like to do without it. Any one of these exercises can help you take a test drive change in your routine.

Creative Thinking
Google created the 80/20 Rule with the intention of boosting innovative thinking. They encouraged employees to dedicate 20 percent of their work time for creative side projects in an effort to encourage innovative output. While it became the butt of jokes for Googlers that it was actually a "120% Rule" (the 20 percent only coming after the 100 percent was given), the concept was a valid one: dedicate time specifically for creative thought.

If you have an employer who gives you time to dedicate to creative endeavors, congratulations! (And use such a gift wisely.)

If, like most, you have an employer who is not as forward thinking, then steal time the best you can. If it can't be 20 percent of your work week (a full 8 hours!) then at least schedule 30 minutes a week (30 minutes a day is better!) to focus on the creative side of your job or to at least spend that time to learn in support of your current role or in preparation for your next job.

If "creative thinking" is something you have not practiced regularly, follow any one or more of these methods listed below to get started:

Anti-Assumption Method: Write down all the assumptions you have around a problem or project. Then go through the list line by line, brainstorming ideas based on the assumptions not being true one at a time.

Connect the Dots Method: Sometimes the magic comes from combining two or more separate ideas together. After brainstorming potential solutions to the problem, try mix and matching common ideas together to produce a new list of potential ideas.

Hypothesis Method: The host summarizes a problem to a small group of advisors who then take turns asking the host questions about the problem. (This should be a straight Q&A, not conversation starters.) With the questions answered, each person then shares a hypothesis or two they have about the problem. Once a list of these hypotheses is made, the host confirms or cancels out each hypothesis. Last, each person gives the host a suggestion for solving the issue.

WHAT'S NEXT

"The afternoon knows what the morning never suspected."
— Robert Frost

A commonly held belief is that two-thirds of all jobs of the future do not even exist today. And by "future" I mean the one that is starting to take shape now and will be the new normal long before we are ready to retire.

Sure, the workplace is changing in large part because of a combination of three main factors: 1) technology, 2) demographics, and 3) globalization.

Technology will continue to have major impacts on the marketplace and workforce. While we can't always know what to expect, we can monitor the trends that help us anticipate what's to come. How might virtual reality, augmented reality, and robotics impact your industry? How might that change your role at the company? How might technological advancements over the next five to 10 years change the way people live, and therefore, change customer behaviors and expectations?

As countries become more connected, the world is becoming increasingly smaller. International relations has a huge impact on business. Political alliances and conflicts are fluid, and economic policies change as each new leader comes to power around the world. How are you preparing for a marketplace that is even more globally connected than today? Conversely, times are increasingly uncertain for international relations. If your assumptions about international political alliances were to turn on its head tomorrow, what would be the potential impact to the company you work for? To your job?

Globalization also points to how diversity between business partners in different countries and co-workers in the same company. As the populations of western countries become increasingly diverse, companies are cognizant that they need to be more sensitive and tolerate of different cultures, generations, and sexual orientations. They must demonstrate a commitment to diversity and inclusion to attract top talent. In turn, employers expect the same of employees, even putting diversity and inclusion behaviors as a line item in annual reviews. What are you doing to become more tolerate and sensitive to people who aren't like you? How do you practice inclusion at work? How are you developing and demonstrating those values professionally?

Last, regardless of all the change that has happened and will happen, no job is permanent. We are all having to prove ourselves day after day to earn our positions, let alone salaries. Regardless of how long we have been with a company or how stable our jobs may seem, any one of us could be looking for a new job tomorrow. Even if we "do everything right." This is both the pro and con of the trend toward a free agent workforce. Your seniority may not help you keep your job, but if you play your cards right, it could help you get contract work, something that may become more important as companies shift toward hiring on fewer full-time employees and more contractors.

What are you doing today to position yourself professionally for the long-run? Or will you take the risk of maintaining the status quo for as long as you can?

In anticipation of more changes to come, will you prepare to grow your career or to accept a severance package?

In ten years, will you look back at today as the turning point for becoming empowered in your career?

You've come too far in your career to hope to fade into the sunset. It is an exciting time as the business world evolves. It is your responsibility to take the challenge to keep your competitive mojo going for years to come.

Dare to be an active participant as a Modern Business Master. The world needs your rich business experience in both the traditional and new ways of doing business.

ABOUT THE AUTHOR

With over 20 years of experience promoting iconic corporate brands, Tracy Darchini has contributed articles about embracing modern business practices to *The Huffington Post*, *Next Avenue*, and *Better After 50*.

By combining her communications experience with her passion for how innovations are changing the way we live and work, Tracy empowers corporate professionals over 40 to pilot their ongoing career growth by building a Forward Thinking Advantage. Tracy believes that her generation is well-positioned for continued success for years to come, provided we are enthusiastically adopting modern business practices.

Tracy lives in Portland, Oregon with her husband and daughter. Connect with Tracy on her blog at *Reflections*.

#ForwardThinkingAdvantage

ACKNOWLEDGEMENTS

With sincere gratitude

To Victor and Anna for their patience and support as I have spent all my off-the-clock hours working on this material for quite some time

To Kathleen and John for always encouraging me to be smart and independent

To Tom and Barbara—one for guiding me more than he knows and the other for guiding me more than I know

To my friends and advisors Anne Carlantone, Lisa Clifford, Tamar Cohen, David Dell, Brad Green, Cami Hamilton, Christine Lohrfink, Karen Otani, and Yai Vargas for supporting me each step of this adventure

To the mentors I have had the privilege of working with and learning from, including Carol Bohdan, Donna Boland, Joyce Fredo, and Patrice Tanaka

/ ACKNOWLEDGEMENTS

To the hundreds of pioneering, creative, and intelligent thought leaders who generously share their knowledge, especially my virtual mentors, David Burkus, Tara Gentile, Marshall Goldsmith, Chris Guillebeau, and Scott Monty

RECOMMENDED RESOURCES

INTRODUCTION

Godin, Seth. *Linchpin: Are You Indispensable?* **Portfolio, 2010. Kindle.**

Schoen, John. **MSNBC News. nbcnews.com, 2013.** https://tinyurl.com/klsf6g5

CHAPTER 1

Goldsmith, Marshall. *Triggers: Creating Behavior That Lasts–Becoming The Person You Want To Be.* **Crown Business, 2015. Kindle.**

CHAPTER 2

Ferriss, Timothy, *The 4 Hour Work Week*. **Harmony, 2009. Kindle.**

Burkus, David, *Under New Management: How Leading Organizations Are Upending Business As Usual*. **Houghton Mifflin Harcourt, 2016. Kindle.**

CHAPTER 3

Henry, Todd. *Die Empty: Unleash Your Best Work Every Day*. **Portfolio, 2013. Kindle.**

CHAPTER 4

Merchant, Nilofer. *11 Rules for Creating Value in the #SocialEra*. **Harvard Business Review Press, 2012. Kindle.**

CHAPTER 5

Hogshead, Sally. *Fascinate: Your 7 Triggers to Persuasion and Captivation*. **HarperCollins Publishers, 2010. Kindle.**

CHAPTER 6

Altucher, James. *The Choose Yourself Guide to Wealth*. Choose Yourself Media LLC, 2015. Kindle.

CHAPTER 7

Gladwell, Malcolm. *Outliers: The Story of Success*. Little, Brown and Company, 2008. Kindle.

WHAT'S NEXT

Tulgan, Bruce. *The Great Generational Shift*. RainmakerThinking, 2017. https://tinyurl.com/lkz9gl6

www.ingramcontent.com/pod-product-compliance
Lightning Source LLC
LaVergne TN
LVHW041549070426
835507LV00011B/1009